i

With love and respect Tony

That Blue Pause

Tony Frisby

ISBN 978 1 54508 250 8

Published by Panda Press
8 BN2 8SR Brighton

Other collections by the author

Letters to the Downs
Letters to the Sea
Letters from a Cave in Saltdean
Unravellings
Me, Me and Not Me - Waterloo Press

Tony Frisby

Having left school at fourteen, Tony Frisby eventually returned to education in England, thirty years after leaving Ireland. With a BA in Art History and MA in Renaissance and Modern Literature from Brunel University, he embarked on a PhD in Northern Irish Poetry. However, soon smitten by the poetic form itself, he abandoned academia to concentrate on writing rather than commenting on poetry.

In Brighton he started a series of poems from and about this, his third place, and in 2011, began collating and re-editing all his work for publication. *Letters to the Sea* was followed by three other collections of *Letters,* and in 2014, Waterloo Press published his ninety-four page poem *Me Me and Not Me.* Guest reader at the 2016 Blackwater International Poetry Festival, he is currently collating three more collections specifically focused on issues of place and displacement which are of intense concern to Frisby, both as poet and as one who, first by necessity, then by force of circumstance, finds himself still living away from 'home'.

Tony reads in venues throughout London and the South East, conducts poetry workshops in public libraries and prison, and edits anthologies for writing groups.

REVIEWS

Letters to the Sea *The Argus* (Brighton), *Pick of the Week*

'…beautifully evocative images. Frisby is unduly modest in his self portrait as a blatherer, a kisser and teller, a floundering wordsmith trawling the depths for inspiration.'

Rosie Clark, poetry critic

Letters to the Downs *The Argus, Pick of the Week*

'…a delight, instantly removing me out into the glorious twin land/seascapes in which we're so lucky to live.'

Kim Protheroe, editor Weekend magazine

Letters to Breda *The Argus*

'…both a metaphor for the pull to record unbidden yet persistent memories, and an evocative tribute to inspiration itself.'

Catherine Meek, poetry critic

Letters from a Cave *The Argus, s*

'Poetry which helps us make sense of the unthinkable.'

Jenny Tregoning, feature writer Weekend magazine

Me, Me and Not Me

'…a work of genius.' John Tatum, broadcaster and poet

ACKNOWLEDGMENTS

I am indebted to all those who support my Face-book page, Tony Frisby Poetry - An Irish Voice in Verse.

Whether positive comment or valued criticism I truly value your feed-back on my work. Thank you all.

Please continue the process with regard to reviewing **That Blue Pause** and with your permission, I will include appropriate remarks in Vol ii of this collection.

Tony

'…human identity is not consistent but is instead a constantly changing assemblage of images and understandings of self.'

Jacques Lacan

DEDICATION

To Dawn

That Blue Pause

Pugilist

[*after the* Boxer of Quirinal - Rome]

Two thousand years since his last fight
yet he remains vigilant,
a fighter glaring at the world
through emptied eyes

that knew the thud of leather,
the dull pale of death.
And though time has aged him
to scarred and bleeding bronze,

and all challengers
stayed in marble, or lost
beneath Rome's inglorious rubble,
that mighty chest still heaves

as he sits, hunched upon his past,
a muscled killing-machine
waiting, staring,
longing for death.

Layerings

All along this hump-backed coast,
milk-white bands of chalk
remind the thundering waves
of ancient connections.

And between each layer
of calcified bone,
dark stripes of brittle flint
mark a vegetable presence

amongst the long gone fish.
Yet, though each stratum differs,
every chalky layer thick as an aeon,
the flint, thin and sharp as knife-slashes

across the cliff's open throat,
all relate the same old truths,
beginnings, endings, love and life
metamorphosed now

into something else: a block of chalk
to write a poem
upon a black welsh slate,
or a broken flint sharp enough

to hone this pencil fit to write
on the blood stained page of history
or scribe a poem to a loved one.
And so, as I knew I would,

I come back to you and me,
for we too are formed in the image
of our past, all beginnings, every ending,
each chunk of life consumed,

layered now on the hinterland
of our smiles. All the hopes,
and heartaches, reflect
in our long-memoried eyes:

each kiss adored, each tear abhorred,
each layer, every seam of chalk
or flint, bed-rocking our place
in the continuum that is love.

Remembering

Sometimes it's the music
of pebbles shifting on the strand,
an evening sky,
the smell of wood-smoke,
a musty, lingering stink of fox
in a cool boreen
and wild woodbine
wandering the lane
that I remember best.

Then again, it might be
the acrid smell of cow shit
or pools of pungent horse piss
on a dusty road,
the economy of sheep tracks,
black loveliness of crows,
the laughter of swifts,
wetness of cloudbursts,
head-lights on the Tramore Road,
Breda Power,
winter nights at Grimspound,
or the heather on Plynlimon
that please me most.

*

But there are times too
when nothing,
not sunset
not dawn
not the strand at Rhossili,
a Norfolk sky or
moonlight on the Wash,

not love on a bicycle
or Beckett at the Tabard,
not Captain Cat's song
– knock twice and ask for Rosie –
not births, pledges, aspirations
nor promises:

nothing,
nothing at all
can satisfy my longing
for the cockle strand
at Woodstown

Stitches in a Tapestry

Feathered tail wagged slow in wonder,
Panda is staring at the crisp, clear reflection
of her Welsh Border Collie perfection,
mirrored in the unflustered surface

of a seaweed-draped rock pool at Saltdean.
Now a paw dips, disturbs the surface
and all is waft, shift, change. And suddenly
it's another now, February 3rd 1959,

and Jimmy Finn is running towards me
as I walk home from Waterford glass factory.
Distressed, thin-voiced, he's screeching,
'Buddy's dead! Poor Buddy's been killed'.

Too old to cry, yet deep sobs rack my voice,
'Oh Jasus, ah what happened to him Jim?
Where is he? Are ye certain he's dead,
sure he's only a puppy?'

'Aw ye feckin eejit,' fumes a red-faced Jimmy,
'Sure I'm talkin' about Buddy Holly,
the American singer, not your mangy scrap of a dog.
Go feck yerself and yer dog, ye ignoramus!'

A few wild punches later, I'm at home,
that mangy scrap of a dog nuzzling my ear...
'til it's waft, shift and change again,
as a splash and whimper from the rock pool

returns me to Panda, to the here, the now
and the where-I-am fifty years on,
a boy-man to-ing and fro-ing between the ages,
a time lord drawn to scenes

and one act plays from a tapestry draped
across the landscape of my thoughts: now in sepia,
now in emerald green, now in mildewed purple,
and now in shimmering black.

A Boreen in County Waterford

Cut me deep, slice these blue-black veins
and the flow of blood will taste of rivers
that brought me from Africa.

Now I am a stick-man on a cave wall,
a drawer of shimmering images which, as the ice melts,
I leave to delight the gaping future.

Find me there, in a bog in Denmark:
note the leather torc, my sacrificed life,
the gold-work around my neck.

Note too my stocky build,
the hair that lines my grinning skull:
its ginger hue still adorns the pates

of my brothers and sisters in the Western Isles.
And though that reign is done,
the world remembers my horned head,

savage axe and Viking tongue,
just as these downs know my lesser sins
and need of solitude.

But only the Celt in me knows
the march of Alba, the ache of conquest,
loss of tongue, the green taste of hunger.

Knows too, Edmund's false charms,
the coffin ships, deaths of heroes,
the double yoke of religion.

And so it is that though my tent
is set upon a foreign coast, it's a boreen
in County Waterford that knows me best.

Hip and haw, old man's beard,
the woodbine smell of honeysuckle,
butter glow of gorse,

remembering the routes already travelled,
memories gathered, sacrifices given, changes made.
And only there is my future known,

there my needs understood, there
amongst the fuchsias dancing
in a boreen in County Waterford.

Saint Bartholomew's Bricks

Hefted solid into place,
that first red, unbuttered brick
is the beginning.
Set it upon itself

and then upon itself again,
and again, until the sky is breached.
Turn some upon a corner
or, with bated breath,

arch a clever few,
to frame a gaping world.
Now add a million brothers,
raise each course with profligate muck,

'til set and squared
against the seasons,
a living art
smiles upon your mastery.

Tough Guys Don't Dance

All sinuous ingratiation,
the poplars on Barnes common
connive with the elements
till equilibrium returns.

The pond-side willows too,
bowing to the windy gods,
practice subservience
and wait for calm to be restored.

Even those rounded downs
once befriended the icy ages,
bartered their high crowns
for shaped and moulded beauty.

Only we, flaccid homo erectus
(clock ticking to earlier doom)
abhor such natural grovelling,
resist all that would form us different

to our own imagined design.

Night Noises

Am I almost there, on the edge of knowing,
a skimming-stone's throw from your depths,
from the thoughts that, murmuring your pillow,
sometimes toss our crumpled bed?

I know your waking beauty,
the buddha soul that, even as the sad world scoffs
behind its lace-net certainties,
drives you endlessly along the route of love.

And you know the waking me,
have learned to love this voice noising your life,
a troubled heart clutching weakly at your lifeline.
Yet still, like gods, we remain enigmas:

me to you, and you to me, even to ourselves.
And so, perched on the edge of what-might-be,
I slyly look upon your sleep,
wondering if you can love me forever,

or if in some catastrophic future
you begin to count my frailties,
the deadened sensibilities which
guiding me thus far helped me survive

amongst the withered bougainvilleas,
you just stop loving me.
What then, and where to go,
should your nerve ends shudder at my touch?

Yet, though horror might await
I still must know what mumbles your dreams
upon our loving-sheets, what thoughts
flood that gentle mind

when the day is done and love has eased your rest
amongst the prancing, dancing, sheep.
Do nightmare endings cloud your dreams
or in imitation of the loving, lusty day,

are they my hands, my lips,
my frantic yearnings that moan your sleep
with muffled incantations
and blessings sighed to the stars?

Unravelling

And if this be about love,
then surely it must begin
with the first you,
the one sitting by the fire

while I kneel at your feet as we unravel
a school jumper I've outgrown.
You're smiling down at me while
dreamlike, I splay my fingers

and with hands apart,
duck and swoop, sway and twist
until skeins of wool fill our basket.
There we are, a pair of sorcerers

unwinding the years, your ears
cocked to the music on Radio Eireann,
my mind galloping between
the task in hand and a ranch in Texas

where a school-boy's hands
are more at home around the butt
of a Colt 45 than unravelling the past.
Now, another vision has you

once again by the fire,
sewing basket by your side, last year's jumper
reduced to memory, balled and ready
to be fashioned anew.

I'm at the kitchen table,
my penny exercise book lies open
and as I chant my nine times table,
you begin your sinless litany,

knit one, purl one, slip a stitch.
Open-mouthed, I'm gawping at the miracle:
the past becoming the present,
and me made warm by the exchange.

The Weather in Saltdean

Only one day, and maybe nothing
much will come of it, but just for one day
it was a different world out there. Now
there's a fresh storm brewing in the east,

another gale lashing our shore.
But that one day, that single sunny day,
was enough to start the earth's clock ticking.
For though we're still in winter's shadow,

the old year's plantings, warmed by that one,
singular day, are already peering
into the gloom, nudging strong
against the rotted dross of autumn. So again,

though March's cantankerous rantings
are yet to be borne, the earth has turned
and new hopes blossom upon
the slowly warming land.

And you've noted a change in me.
Like the soil, my icy mood has thawed,
there's a bounce in my walk,
a spade in my hands.

It's as though, despite that one glorious day
at the back end of February,
the spring might need my help.
So I prod and nudge,

dig and tease, tweak a little here,
prune a little there, in wild imaginings
of what will grow again
one day. One day soon.

Paddy Brown's Long Road

Far away
and long before we met,
I fell in love.
I was only a boy,

but on dark evenings
we'd meet on the corner
of Paddy Brown's Long Road
and make love in the hedgerow.

Afterwards, we'd cry,
then she'd cycle home
to her family and I'd walk
back to Cannon Street

then fret until I fell asleep.
I only remember these things because,
when you kissed me just now
I almost whispered her name.

Nostalgia

'Have a nice day' days,
bar-codes and zip-codes

the hurry-up muzak of supermarkets
and splash-back of beer-cans

have me pining
for laid-back days

when our schoolboy tents
flapped gently

all summer long

at Stradbally.

Horizontal Jogging

Tomorrow
best
describes
my
philosophical
bent,
and
my
tendency
towards
indolence
is
pronounced
before
a
roaring
fire.
You
however,
can
increase
my
tempo
at
any
time:
just
one
smile
or
your
hand

gently
brushing
my
hair,
guaranteeing
that
I
will
always
rise
to
the
occasion.

I Never Go There...

never tend the flowers,
never rip the clogging weeds
from sacred places, never make the journey,
never visit the graves of my dead.

But we meet, and though scattered
to seven corners of the earth,
it's an ever-growing entourage
of souls and spirits that gathers

on Whiteway Lane to talk, reminisce,
to laugh, to console
as we set out together walking
the gentle hills above Saltdean,

a man, his loved ones,
friends and relations
strolling the ups and downs
of a shared and cherished past.

But what to make of those stragglers,
that group shuffling in the wake
of our procession.
What to do, or say? How to act?

How to deal with those drowned children,
their frantic parents,
all searching amongst my dead
for comfort? How to tell them

that their tear-soaked cortège
winds a different route to mine;
that theirs,
beginning in a nightmare

ends not in a gentle walk
but in rubber death-traps
that floundered on a sea
of mistrust and usury?

Sad Day Blues

I need sad days to write sad words
and deaths to rhyme of death

floods to speak of horrid waves
and the drowning of children

the nothingness of floating dolls
and blinded fools upon the heath

fill my mind.

To Feed or Not to Feed the Monster

Another new year
and, in honour of the occasion,
a mobile phone company
is offering me a large discount

to ditch last new year's 'must have' phone
for this new year's 'must have'
all knowing, all hearing,
indestructible model.

But they caught me in a good mood
so, resisting the temptation
to swap what worked
for something else that works,

I sent the money instead
to the nurse who tended to my Mother
whose voice I miss
more than anything I've ever owned.

If She Were

If she were silence, she would be
the fall of snow on snow,

the hushed bloomings
in the buds of spring,

that blue pause
between the evening

and a setting sun.

That Light

[after *Van Gogh's* The Potato Eaters]

No luncheon rendezvous this,
no fatted gourmets gorge at this thin table.
No royal portraits these, no kings or queens
in bright prismatic colour
to please posterity's eyes.

No sunflowered field in sun-drenched Arles,

but the crows are here, those black
and terrifying nightmares, destined soon
to swoop and squawk the southern cornfields
of his mind, stalking now the future,
in cobwebbed corners
of this cramped hut in the flat cold north.

But there is light,

that sturdy oil lamp confining the crows,
his growing despair, to benign invisibility
within the room's softest shadows,
shining brightest upon those who dine in this,
his soft intrusion into the world of poverty.

And there is love,

in every glance, gesture and smile,
in each and every shaft of light,
in all those sad,
knowing brushstrokes.

Twinkling Seas

It's the last day of October yet Saltdean beach
still boasts a colourful scattering
of semi-naked sun worshippers.

Just out of their depth, a group of teenagers
are noisily coming of age
in the twinkling sea,

while among the rock-pools, toddlers and parents
wield toy fishing nets in the gentle glow
of this late, late, Indian summer.

(It's like a dream:
as though the elements
have turned their backs
on the whims
of clock-watching seasons,
and opted instead
for soft breezes,
warm seas and balmy sunsets
to bring this dire year
to a gentler close.

It's as though the gods and dogs of war
have gone to rest
and in their absence
we, the led, have downed
our killing tools
to laugh and play together
in a mythic sun.)

But all games end, and the first day of November
is at odds with yesterday's gentler times
as raw winds from the east return to tease
the sea to anger and the tempting divide
between earth and the stars mutates
from beckoning promise to monochrome, saddened grey.

Shameless pen, arrogant dream,
this concoct of deceit,
this unworthy conjuring of a scene
to dazzle the blood-stained truth
with worthless hope:
for the gods of war never rest
but are awake and snarling in the east.

Netherlands

[i]

Tulip days, warm nights,
floating streets
flying bridges:

the land
stretching
flat and safe

you and I
stretching
flat and catty-cornered

on a shipwrecked
bed
in Amersfoort.

[ii]

Later,
I wag
a protestant finger
at Mondrian's
ghostly apparition
for smoking
a fag
in the family home,
in Amersfoort.

Different Times Different Games

It's autumn and the streetlights
on Cannon Street are glowing wistful
in the damp evening air.
Anne Forsey and Brenda Power

giggle secretly on the corner
of Gracedieu Road,
and near Paddy Kinsella's house
a couple of corner-boys while their time

eyeing the girls and wondering
if what they say about Brenda is true.
Oblivious to such grown-up mysteries,
Studs Mull, Dixie Maloney,

Brenda's little brother Fintan
and meself are skipping and bawling
around the lamp-post
outside Mrs Mull's huckster shop

ignoring our Da's angry shouts
to get back indoors
so the ould ones can have
a bit of peace and quiet.

*

Autumn in Mosul
but only the dogs of war can play:
no quiet or peace in Aleppo,
for the dogs of war must play.

Sac Eile Móna   (Another Sack of Turf)

Is fada an bóthar
ón Trá Ar ais ag Trá Mhór

leis na haillte bána ag Black Rock.
Agus is leor in aghaidh na bliana

ós rud é codlata ceann a scannáin ladhar
agus cowboy

ag Ma Crosby ar Coliseum Pictiúrlann
aice Túr Raghnaill.

Ach tá sé aon turas ar chor ar bith
i mo shúil aigne; sa-am a thógann sé

a mheabhrú Uncail Micky i bPort Lách,
Is féidir liom a bheith ann agus ar ais le sac eile

a móna fearr triomaithe
téamh an ruacain mo chroí.

Another Sack of Turf   (Sac Eile Móna)

It's a long road
from the Back Strand at Tramore

to the white cliffs at Black Rock.
And it's many a year

since sleeping head to toe
and cowboy films

at Ma Crosby's Coliseum Cinema
near Reginald's Tower.

But it's no journey at all
in my mind's eye, for in the time it takes

to remember Uncle Micky in Portlaw,
I can be there and back

with another sack of his best dried turf,
warming the cockles of my heart.

Rasta-Christ

(after a painting by Vincent Donlin)

i

Trust me, he said, 'Je suis artist!'
and his dictum – paraphrased –
echoed down the isms,
'Paint is paint is paint.'

And the message triumphed
and the words became the deed.
Nothing changes, nothing
metamorphoses upon itself:

not Manet's temptress,
that scrubbed courtyard in Delft,
not Giotto's tender dead Saint Francis,
or Leonardo's smirking lady-man.

All remain as paint,
mere blendings of colour and genius
that sorcer the mind's delighted eye
to hail a shadow as enough.

ii

But when that Rasta-Christ smiled,
the understood retreated and I believed again

in the mysterious transmogrification
of colour into new reality:

that black and risen saviour,
that high stepping Rasta-Christ

strutting his two thousand years of fame
on canvas thin as the blink of an eye.

Shooting Stars

It was a few days before the winter solstice
when we walked the midnight beach at Saltdean
looking for shooting stars.

But I became so entranced
by the heaving waves unwillingness
to communicate with anything

other than their own tumbling forms,
that I barely registered your comment
about the shooting star you'd spotted.

Yet though I missed that star's bright flash,
later I did spot what appeared to be two people
moving amongst sea-weed strewn rocks,

near the cave where we'd seen a couple
holding hands and laughing in the spring.
I made no immediate connection between the couple,

that shooting star and the forms among the rocks,
but now, with Christmas edging closer,
I've started to wonder. What, I find myself asking,

what if the star was some kind of portent,
a sign for us to follow, the ghostly visions
on the rocks a guide,

the cave a place for new beginnings,
a fresh start? One brave imaginative leap
into a future where hope and compassion

flood the earth, the seas run clear,
uncontaminated, and only shooting stars
rule the heavens?

17997378R00034

Printed in Poland
by Amazon Fulfillment
Poland Sp. z o.o., Wrocław